Experiencing God's Grace With Affirmations

Teresa Ngene and Rabia Wood

Experiencing God's Grace With Affirmations

Teresa Ngene and Rabia Wood

Teresa Ngene and Rabia Wood

Experiencing Gods Grace

Copyright © 2021 by Teresa Ngene and Rabia Wood.

All rights reserved.

No part of this book may be reproduced or transmitted in any form or by any means, electronic or mechanical, including photo copying, recording, or by any information storage and retrieval system, without permission in writing from the copyright author, except for the use of brief quotations in a book review.

Library of Congress Cataloging–In– Publication Data

Name: Ngene, Teresa/Wood, Rabia, author.

Title: Experiencing God's Grace With Affirmations/Ngene, Teresa and Wood, Rabia

Identifiers:
LCCN: 2021913011
ISBN: 978-1-970135-92-3 paperback
        978-1-63960-000-7 ebook

Published in the United States by Pen2Pad Ink Publishing.

All scriptural quotations are taken from the King James and New Living Translation Versions of the Bible.

Requests to publish work from this book or to contact the author should be sent to:
teresangene5@gmail.com or rabiasmith@me.com

Teresa Ngene and Rabia Wood

Book Dedication

This book is dedicated to our dear friend and spiritual son, Tafadzwa Soda. Thank you for believing and supporting our ministry. You are truly missed.

We also dedicate this book to our families for being supportive and understanding of this arduous process. We love you.

Teresa Ngene and Rabia Wood

A Letter for You

Dearest Reader,

Thank you for purchasing our book. We wrote it to shed light on things that could affect your growth. The Holy Spirit makes everything plain and reminds you of all things God has told you. He is the parting gift of *peace*. (John 14:26 AMP)

Each of us has struggled with some form of rejection. We may not look or act like it, but it happened. In our quiet moments, we had to face some form of self-doubt. There is a lot of pressure in this world to hold everything together: to look like we "have it going on" when inside we are a complete mess.

This book will show you three different views that affect our growth: The World View, The Self View, and God's View. Our hope and prayer is that you exercise these affirmations so that your spirit will connect with what God has said about you. This is the truth. The Word of God is a mirror. It reflects who you really are. (James 1:22-24 TPT) God is not a man that He should lie. (Numbers 23:19 KJV)

May God bless you and keep you always.

Rabia & Teresa

Teresa Ngene and Rabia Wood

What are Affirmations?

Affirmations are words that are spoken by God about you and or your situation. The Word of God, however, must be rooted in your heart. One way to do this by saying affirmations. Death and life are in the power of the tongue. (Proverbs 18:20-21 KJV) You either bless or curse with your mouth. When you are born again, the Holy Spirit will dwell inside you. The Holy Spirit is the *power* of God. The Holy Spirit becomes your power source.

Why use Affirmations?

We use affirmations to change our situation, perception, atmosphere, attitude, mindset, and/or emotions. Your words shape your world. It is like having our own personal cheerleader sent by **HIM** into your life. These words come alive and manifest themselves in how you walk, talk, and breathe every single day.

Who can use Affirmations?

Born again Christians (also known as a New Creation) can use affirmations. These words of love and truth are for anyone who accepts Christ as their Savior. If you believe that

Jesus Christ was born, crucified, died, buried, and rose again for our sins, affirmations were created specifically for you to use to navigate in the earthly realm and continue moving forward in the earthly realm. It's like 2 Corinthians 5:17 (NIV) says, "Therefore, if anyone is in Christ, the new creation has come: The old is gone, the new is here!"

How do we use Affirmations?

The process to use affirmations effectively is quite simple:

1. Choose an affirmation that addresses how you are feeling or your situation.

2. Look in the mirror.

3. Say affirmation out loud.

4. Repeat the affirmation until you believe it.

The power of the Holy Spirit will convict your heart. Then, peace and joy will be restored. God is not man. HE does not lie. HIS words are always true.

The Views

The following are the perspectives this book will explain in order for you to understand the importance of each affirmation.

World View

This view is how we view reality and make sense of our lives and the world. It's our set of beliefs and how we express ourselves culturally and explain our experiences. This includes your family background and culture.

Self-View

Self - view is what we believe is real regardless if it is conscious or subconscious. It is the driving force behind every emotion, decision, and action. It affects our response to every area of life. It's the idea we have about who are physically, emotionally, socially, and spiritually. It includes our thoughts, preferences, habits, hobbies, skills, and areas of weakness.

God's View

God's perspective is different from ours. So, God's view is what HE wants us to know and understand about our experiences. He has the entire picture where we only see a piece of the puzzle. Since HE has the entire picture, HIS view will fill in the missing pieces to our puzzle of life. HE made us in HIS image. HE has a plan and purpose for our lives.

Day 1

World View

Life is a tumultuous journey. There will never be a "perfect" situation or relationship. We will get rejected. We will get criticized. We will experience unnecessary pain no matter how much we attempt to avoid it. This is when our Survival Mode switch kicks ON: holding in breath, clenching our jaws, creating migraines, causing stress in our shoulders. We do not take inventory of the positives happening. We are just waiting for the next blow.

Self-View

For the first time in my life, I was truly grieving. The loss of my marriage. I was a wife for 20 years. Since I did not experience true grief before, I had to develop my own process. I couldn't look to my mother to figure out what worked for me. I needed a way that helped me deal with my feelings and thoughts instead of walking around holding my breath waiting for "it" to pass.

God's View

Please say the following affirmation:

I decree that my set time of favor shall NOT be frustrated in Jesus' name!

Bible Verse to Remember: Psalm 102:13 (TPT)

I know you are about to arise and show your tender love to Zion. Now is the time, Lord, for your compassion and mercy to be poured out; the appointed time has come for your prophetic promises to be fulfilled!

Day 2

World View

Scary movies are scary because of the dread directors, actors, and writers cultivate from the beginning to the end of the film. They want us to be afraid of the unknown, and most of us fall for it all the time. So, when natural disasters, political scandals, and desecrations of holy grounds happen, we feel the same type of dread. We wonder if this is really where we need to be.

Self-View

Dread. It consumes me in the pit of my stomach. I lay in the dark and allow the waves of dread to course through my veins. Warm teardrops run down the side of my eyes and drip onto my pillow. I feel regret. As a matter of fact, it is deep regret that instantly echoes in my spirit. Then, I sit up in the dark. I wipe my face. I slowly slip out of bed making sure my footsteps are not heard. I need my comfort. My heart is racing. I must find this scripture that is echoing in my inner parts: Psalm 37. I begin to worship. I am reminded of who I am and what I have been commissioned to do: flaws and all. I am qualified by Him. My spirit is settled. All is well. This is my reality. The lesson is simple: never allow yourself to stay in a dark place. Confessions are a lifestyle. This is my truth, and I live it daily.

God's View

Please say the following affirmation:

I will not look back and return to the old. Father, cause me to ascend to new realms of power and new realms of authority! Grant me access to new levels of divine revelation!

Bible Verse to Remember: Psalm 37: 24 (TPT)

If they stumble badly they will still survive, for the Lord lifts them up with his hands.

Day 3

World View

We all have that button: the button that causes us to act besides ourselves. Anger is an accepted emotion in this world. People enjoy watching and experiencing anger for the drama that comes with it. It can make you feel incredibly high and powerful while simultaneously leaving you at its mercy and unpredictability.

Self-View

These past few years have been the most difficult. Past hurts keep reappearing. I know what the Word of God says. I thought I forgave my mother and father, but I haven't. Layers of pain stack up one on top of the other. Anger and rage consume my very core. I believed the lie that forgiving took away the pain. What I forgot is what feeling pain does for me. Feeling pain means that I am alive. I depend on God and not my own strength. As soon as I take my eyes off God and put it on myself, I am on my own. The enemy wants us to be narcissistic: use our own strength, power, and wisdom like a one-man army. If we are alone, there is less of a battle.

God's View

Please say the following affirmation:

I pull down strongholds. I cast out vain imagination and everything that exalts itself against the knowledge of Jesus Christ. My thoughts are subject to the Lordship of Christ in Jesus' name.

Bible Verse to Remember: 2 Corinthians 10:5 (TPT)

We can demolish every deceptive fantasy that opposes God and break through every arrogant attitude that is raised up in defiance of the true knowledge of God. We capture, like prisoners of war, every thought and insist that it bow in obedience to the Anointed One.

Day 4

World View

Will the bill get paid? Will I get the job? Will she really like me? All are questions of the unknown. All are questions of worry. Worry can make your mind dwell on difficulty or troubles because worry focuses on the unknown. We live in a world that wants to know everything. EVERYTHING.

Self-View

I woke up in a funk that I could not seem to shake. I was walking out to my car to go to lunch. My life was a mess. My finances were a mess. My marriage was a mess. In my heart, I talked to God.

"Lord? When? When are all these promises that you showed me going to happen? I'm tired of worrying!" I asked.

"Did I tell you to worry? No. I told you to cast your cares on Me." HE answered.

Two voices tend to rear their ugly heads at the wrong times: your voice and the enemy's voice. Your voice is driven by your emotions. Emotions are in place to protect us. The enemy's voice gives anxiety, worry, and doubt. It is contrary to the Word of God.

God's View

Please say the following affirmation:

No more distracting, disturbing, and destructive measures. Jesus was sent here to destroy the works of the enemy, so I have no reason to worry.

Bible Verse to Remember: I John 3:8 (TPT)

But the one who indulges in a sinful life is of the devil, because the devil has been sinning from the beginning. The reason the Son of God was revealed was to undo and destroy the works of the devil.

Day 5

World View

What is your limit? Your boundary? Personal boundaries are guidelines, rules, or limits that a person creates to identify reasonable, safe, and permissible ways for other people to behave towards them. It also shapes how they will respond when someone passes those limits. Society will lead you to believe that boundaries are unnecessary: the more we know of you, the more we will like you. Setting boundaries will often bring criticism from others because it makes them uncomfortable.

Self-View

When you make a behavior change or boundary move, you begin the game of emotional checkers: the other person will make a counter move in response to what you do. They will attempt to get you back. For example, they may say "You always make it about you!" Wow. That is a nice counter move that will hit you in the gut! You begin to think that maybe you do make everything about yourself. However, you have to remember that it is about persevering and protecting yourself. It is about creating a safe space. Creating boundaries can initially create anxiety. For me, I have had to reinforce these boundaries. I am completely unapologetic about protecting myself. No one can make me feel any type of way unless I allow it.

God's View

Please say the following affirmation:

Father, grant me strategies to identify, resist, overcome and overthrow every plot and plan that is set up for my demise. I shall not be ignorant of the enemies' devices!

Bible Verse to Remember: I John 3:8 (TPT)

But the one who indulges in a sinful life is of the devil, because the devil has been sinning from the beginning. The reason the Son of God was revealed was to undo and destroy the works of the devil.

Day 6

World View

If you have a problem money can fix, you are good. There are people with more money than they could ever imagine, but they cannot buy health or happiness. Steve Jobs had all the money in the world, and it could not save his life. The world will tell you that money is the key to happiness while being the root of all evil. Still, we steal, kill, lie, and everything else possible just to have a few coins or dollars in our pocket.

Self-View

I went through a divorce recently. Many parts of my life were affected, but my finances were the worst. I thought I would have to uproot my children from the only home they had ever known. I realized that this was the best problem that we could have. It helped me to appreciate our health and wealth in each other.

God's View

Please say the following affirmation:

I come against the spirit of deprivation. The Lord prospers the works of my hands.

Bible Verse to Remember: Psalm 37: 25 (TPT)

I was once inexperienced, but now I'm old. Not once have I found a lover of God forsaken by him, nor have any of their children gone hungry.

Day 7

World View

Self-esteem is confidence in one's own worth or abilities. You would think self-esteem would not be a world issue. Yes, it is. Technically, no one is supposed to control it but you. However, bullying, popular opinion, and social media cultivate and curate the opinion we have of others and the opinion we have of ourselves. We are constantly attempting to be like someone else because we do not know how to be ourselves.

Self-View

It's the filter over our eyes that distorts the vision of ourselves because of how people made us feel. Words. So carelessly spoken. The beatings are long forgotten. The scars are fading. They are a reminder of so long ago, but the words still ring "true". They are an echo in a wounded soul; Echoed off the lies bouncing around in our heads. Lies. Now the real work begins. Who am I? Really?

God's View

Please say the following affirmation:

*I lift any **FALSE** burdens. I remove feelings of heaviness, oppression, and depression. I give it to the Lord who sustains me. I shall not be moved in Jesus' name.*

Bible Verse to Remember: Ephesians 6: 13 (TPT)

Because of this, you must wear all the armor that God provides so you're protected as you confront the slanderer for you are destined for all things and will rise victorious.

Day 8

World View

Baseball Catchers. Medieval knights. Doctors. What do all of these careers have in common? They wear some type of armor. It is a protective covering used as a defense against weapons. When a person wears armor, it deflects or absorbs the impact of other weapons. Soldiers go into battle wearing their full armor to sustain their life in order to win the battle. Without armor, you will sustain wounds and feel pain that could have been prevented.

Self-View

When you put on the whole armor of God, you will be able to stand your ground. You will not succumb to fear regardless of what happens around you. I have had miserable moments when my mind would go into overdrive. I forgot I had the most powerful sword: the **Word of God**. One of the enemy's strategies is to wear us out. He desires to keep us busy. This is why we receive attack after attack after attack. I got really angry and stubborn! I refused to stay down. Enough was enough! It was time for war!

Don't give in or out! WEAR THE DEVIL OUT! Resist him, and he will flee from you. How do you resist him? Use the Word of God. Use the whole armor of God to put Satan where he belongs: under your feet! Glory to God!

God's View

Please say the following affirmation:

Father, I thank You for the instructions You have given me in Your Word. Your Word is life to me. It is where I draw my strength. I am fully suited up with the whole armor of God. I am steadfast, unwavering, firmly rooted, and unmovable in the face of adversity. The wiles, tactics, manipulations, and strategies of the devil are rendered futile in Jesus' name.

Bible Verse to Remember: James 4:7 (AMP)

So submit to [the authority of] God. Resist the devil [stand firm against him] and he will flee from you.

Day 9

World View

There have been many instances on television and the news where someone did something that was physically impossible, and they don't remember performing the act. That is because their endorphins took over so they could do this amazing act. Endorphins usually diminish our ability to see, hear, or become aware of pain. Staying busy and surrounding ourselves with people can be used in the same way. Many times we stay busy or surround ourselves with people and activities to desensitize the pain we feel. The people and activities act as endorphins.

Self-View

Some of us are afraid to be alone. We are not comfortable with their own company. We entertain ourselves with things we KNOW are not good for us. Endorphins spike. We settle and get comfortable. We endure. Why? Is it for a moment of bliss? Is it a band aid fix? All of those things are temporary.

Reality sets in. We wrestle. We were made for so much more. He shows us glimpses of the possibilities. Yay! God was so precise when He created you. Everything was on purpose. Nothing is broken.

God's View

Please say the following affirmation:

Father I thank you for the living Word. It shows me who I really am and how to have joy in the midst of pain. No matter what happens, my hope and joy is in you.

Bible Verse to Remember: Hebrews 4:12 (TPT)

For we have the living Word of God, which is full of energy, like a two-mouthed sword. It will even penetrate to the very core of our being where soul and spirit, bone and marrow meet! It interprets and reveals the true thoughts and secret motives of our hearts.

Day 10

World View

Freedom is "the power or right to act, speak, or think without being held back". We limit ourselves because of fear, lack of knowledge, or we forget our rights. Although we have freedom, we don't always make choices like we do.

Self-View

I spoke to myself one day and said the following: "Rabia. Stop living like you are dead. Jesus died for you. You are walking in freedom. Greater things are to come!" I used to feel like I wasted so much time looking for perfection. I had this overwhelming need to be perfect, right, and number one.

I was not living. I was existing because I was bracing myself for the next blow. I walked through life with a clenched jaw, tense shoulders, defenses up, impenetrable, numb, angry, critical, miserable, and pretending. All because I lacked love for myself.

God's View

Please say the following affirmation:

I refuse to be limited! I see possibilities. I see success. I see victory. I see these virtues only!

Bible Verse to Remember: Psalm 147:11 (KJV)

The Lord taketh pleasure in them that fear him, in those that hope in His mercy.

Day 11

World View

Creation is "the action or process of bringing something into existence". It is taking something from your thoughts to a physical representation like a hair stylist with a new hairstyle or the fashion designer each spring with the latest fashion. Sometimes our fear of who we really are keeps us from taking an idea from our mind to something real.

Self-View

I used to believe the lie that I was not enough. My family culture based my value on my physical appearance. Growing up, I had four sisters who were very skinny, and I was severely overweight. I wasted so much time on what they thought of me. When in reality, I was more valuable than any jewel.

God's View

Please say the following affirmation:

My life is for the Glory of God. I am on a journey on preordained pathways! No matter what happens, I will square up, chin up, and be conscious that the Father of our Lord Jesus Christ has established and preordained me!

Bible Verse to Remember: Romans 8:29 (NLT)

For God knew his people in advance, and he chose them to become like his Son, so that his Son would be the firstborn among many brothers and sisters.

Day 12

World View

Surprise! Surprises tend to reveal that which is a secret. It's like you are unveiling or removing a covering. It's scary to think that something is being kept from you, but it is. You do not know everything. Unfortunately, some things are being kept from you for reasons that you cannot control. Whether you like to believe it or not, there are mysteries that you will never uncover thanks to the nature of this world.

Self-View

When I became a born-again Christian, many things were not clear to me. I did not know my purpose. I would wrestle with myself. I did not know how to navigate my new-found freedom. I knew with head knowledge that there was freedom in Christ. I wanted somebody to tell me exactly what to do. Over time, I learned that submitting to God in totality would create in me a new-found freedom: I belong to

Him alone.

God's View

Please say the following affirmation:

I will never stumble or walk in confusion. The Word of God is a lamp to my feet and a light to my path. My path is a shining light that shines brighter and brighter unto the perfect day.

Bible Verse to Remember: John 16:13 (TPT)

But when the truth-giving Spirit comes, he will unveil the reality of every truth within you. He won't speak his own message, but only what he hears from the Father, and he will prophetically reveal to you what is to come.

Day 13

World View

Self-condemnation is the blaming of yourself for something. It is like an admission of failure. Some examples include the following: "Oh, I messed up so bad.", "I should have done this.", "Why didn't I do this?", "I knew this was going to happen." Today's society usually accepts this form of negativity because you choose to ridicule yourself before anyone has the chance to do it and hurt you.

Self-View

I have done many things wrong in my life. I lied. I cheated. I made a lot of mistakes. I can truly say I did not like myself. Anger was my go to emotion, and I wielded my words like a sword. I was proud of the fact that I was able to crush someone with them. It made me feel powerful. The power that was robbed from me from an early age was restored when I yielded my 'sword'.

God's View

Please say the following affirmation:

I reign and rule in life as a ruler because the gift of righteousness is LAVISHLY bestowed upon me!

Bible Verse to Remember: Romans 4:5-6 (TPT)

But no one earns God's righteousness. It can only be transferred when we no longer rely on our own works, but believe in the one who powerfully declares the ungodly to be righteous in his eyes. It is faith that transfers God's righteousness into your account! Even King David himself speaks to us regarding the complete wholeness that comes inside a person when God's powerful declaration of righteousness is heard over our life. Apart from our works, God's work is enough.

Day 14

World View

Sometimes in life you have to endure something challenging to get to a victory. When you graduate from school you have endured some challenging classes to get the diploma. To endure something is "to experience an unpleasant or difficult process or situation without giving up". Think of it like going to the dentist, getting an annual mammography, or any annual visit that is uncomfortable.

Self-View

I have been in relationships where I have had to endure silence and or anger due to preserving someone else's feelings or trying to preserve the relationship. Many of us do this daily where we suffer in silence.

God's View

Please say the following affirmation:

Father I thank you that I am no longer a slave to my fears or opinion of others. Everything I do is unto you. I know that I can trust you to lead me through heartbreak, trauma, and the issues of life.

Bible Verse to Remember: Romans 4:5 (TPT)

But no one earns God's righteousness. It can only be transferred when we no longer rely on our own works, but believe in the one who powerfully declares the ungodly to be righteous in his eyes. It is faith that transfers God's righteousness into your account!

Day 15

World View

Death of a loved one. Major illness such as a stroke. Covid-19. All are life altering circumstances. These are events or facts that cause something undesirable to happen. It changes your life for better or worse (usually worse).In order to move forward, you have to learn a new set of rules and way of thinking.

Self-View

You know that painful, life-altering circumstance you keep asking God to please hurry up and fix? Well, you aren't alone in wanting these things to be different. Even Jesus asked the Father to change His circumstance and fix what He could fix in an instant! When Jesus was arrested and eventually, He said: "Abba, Father, everything is possible for you. Take this cup from me!" If I'm honest, I feel the same way sometimes.

God's View

Please say the following affirmation:

Father, I am inspired more than ever to do Your will and fulfill my ministry in You! I thank You for opening my understanding to my abilities in Christ. I will accomplish all things through the power of the Holy Spirit.

Bible Verse to Remember: Jeremiah 29:11 (NIV)

For I know the plans I have for you," declares the Lord, "plans to prosper you and not to harm you, plans to give you hope and a future.

Day 16

World View

A wound is defined as "an injury to living tissue caused by a cut, blow or other impact, typically one in which the skin is cut or broken." Wounds can be categorized in a number of different ways. There are 6 types of wounds: Incised, Laceration, Abrasion, Puncture, Avulsion and Amputation. Most people in the world don't understand why Christians are Christians. They see it as pointless. "Why suffer?" They say. "What's the point of being saved if you can still be wounded?"

Self-View

Soulish wounds will mislead you into entertaining things or people you would not ordinarily entertain. I remember wanting to be accepted so bad. I wanted people to understand me. I became close to people who did not fill the wounds. Instead, they made me feel worse. No human being can fill any void that you have. Time does not heal all wounds.

God's View

As believers, the bible teaches that we would have a life of trials and tribulations, but it is a life of overcoming. Jesus promised us that because He overcame the world, so would we. No matter what the storm, we are victorious through Christ Jesus.

Please say the following affirmation:

Father, I thank You for making me white as snow. Thank You that I am washed clean by the Blood of the Lamb. Burn up my impurities. Get rid of anything that does not please You.

Bible Verse to Remember: Isaiah 1:25 (NIV)

I will turn my hand against you; I will thoroughly purge away your dross and remove all your impurities.

Day 17

World View

To be crafty means "to be clever at achieving one's goal by deceitful methods". Craftiness is considered to be a skill especially in business. In most relationships, it's about how you can use a person to help you achieve more financially.

Self-View

"As soon as I take my eyes off God and shift to self, I'm on my own." - Rabia Wood.

The enemy wants you to look at yourself, your strength, your power, your works, your abilities, your education, your "wisdom": A one-man army. The enemy is so crafty and subtle. Winning to me is winning one situation at a time. Winning is conquering one encounter at a time. Winning is facing one trigger at a time. It is telling me that I won the battle today.

God's View

Please say the following affirmation:

Your mercies are new every day! We won the war! Jesus did it! We are victorious! We are NOT trying to be!

Bible Verse to Remember: Lamentations 3:22-23 (NLT)

The faithful love of the Lord never ends! His mercies never cease. Great is His faithfulness; His mercies begin afresh each morning.

Day 18

World View

Acceptance means to be received as adequate or suitable like being admitted into a group. Acceptance is a human need. We require it. It makes us feel we are part of something. Transparency, to be able to be viewed, is not something that happens a lot in society. Many people refrain from being truly transparent due to trust, judgement, and fear of rejection.

Self-View

"Transparency with the absence of wisdom will get you played." - Rabia Wood.

When you want so desperately to be heard, you overshare. When you want to be understood, you overshare. You open yourself up to being mishandled. You trust people when you should not have. When love equates acceptance for you, you overshare. You want to give folks insight into your reality. Close your mouth. They are not going to get you anyway. You have become naked and vulnerable with too many folks.

God's View

Please say the following affirmation:

(Insert Your Name): I accept your flaws. I accept my imperfections. I accept everything about me. What I can't change, I accept. I love you, (Insert Your Name).

Bible Verse to Remember: James 1:5 (TPT)

And if anyone longs to be wise, ask God for wisdom and he will give it! He won't see your lack of wisdom as an opportunity to scold you over your failures but he will overwhelm your failures with his generous grace.

Day 19

World View

Spring, Summer, Fall, Winter. We all know those seasons. We dress differently. We act differently. We adjust ourselves in order to accommodate the climate, and it does not make us uncomfortable. Spiritual seasons are different times in our lives that teach us lessons on strength, endurance, growth, faith, and trust. How you handle the spiritual seasons depends on your ability to be strong, have faith, grow, endure, and trust His process. However, this world wants you to focus more on yourself than your relationship with Him. Depending on God means you will not depend on yourself.

Self-View

Life is measured in seasons. In some seasons of our lives, we meet people when we are in a broken space. We meet people when we are in the midst of trauma, and we are not functioning in our full capacity. In our vulnerability, we overshare. We become too transparent. So, they put labels on us. They put us in a box. They think they know us. They anticipate our moves. They anticipate our responses. Our reactions are our answers.

God's View

Please say the following affirmation:

Father, all I need is You and You alone. You alone are my portion. There is nothing impossible with You.

Bible Verse to Remember: James 3:2 (TPT)

We all fail in many areas, but especially with our words. Yet if we're able to bridle the words we say we are powerful enough to control ourselves in every way, and that means our character is mature and fully developed.

DAY 20

World View

Provision means to provide a supply of something. Society is great at helping in storms such as tornadoes, floods, and any other natural disaster. However, when a personal trauma happens, society tries to talk you through it based on their experiences and or knowledge. Unfortunately, they are ill equipped to bring lasting healing and eternal joy.

Self-View

I used to believe the lie that to measure progress I HAD to be perfect. I had to have the appropriate responses to situations every time. I would beat myself up if I resorted to old patterns. I would look for validation from people I respected just to justify myself. I placed unnecessary pressure on myself. People would always have an opinion on how I should handle a situation.

I serve a PERFECT God, who has made provision for these moments. He is a God who is not surprised by anything that I do and will do. He has extended His grace every time.

God's View

Please SING the following affirmation:

> *Ohhhh, You have my Heart!*
> *Ohhhh, You have my Heart!*

> *Be the Lord of my emotions! Set me free from selfish motives. Search me until there is nothing hidden! I will give You everything! Speak Lord of my emotions!*

Bible Verse to Remember: Psalm 42:1 (TPT)

I long to drink of you, O God, to drink deeply from the streams of pleasure flowing from your presence. My longings overwhelm me for more of you.

Day 21

World View

An overcomer is someone who succeeds in dealing with some problem or difficulty or a person who succeeds in gaining control of some problem or difficulty. Some ways society attempts to overcome problems without God's help is excessive behaviors such as binging on food, alcohol, drugs, sex, etc.

Self-View

Secrets and shame weight on these shoulders that I never asked for. Oppressors are old or dead. I am no longer dependent on them. I am no longer seeking shelter from them. I see them for the true boogeyman that they are. I'm told to keep those secrets of old. Protect the old. Honor the legacy. Legacy you say? Legacy of what? Oppression? When is it my time? When is it my time to be free? When can I really live?

Didn't Christ come so I can live this abundant life? So why do I still feel enslaved?

The war/slavery is raging within my spirit. Who will win? Who will win is the one that is most dominant within me. If it's flesh, then flesh will win. Then, I will succumb to the lie that I am a secret keeper. I hold others to shame. If it's the spirit, I will push past flesh so when I am weak, He is strong.

What will you choose today? Will you turn to the one who knit your innermost parts? Get on your knees and cry out to Him? He is the only one who can bring true and lasting healing. Try Him today.

God's View

Please say the following affirmation:

I am an Overcomer! I meditate on the Word day and night until it takes over my thought process! In Jesus name!

Bible Verse to Remember: I John 5:4-5 (ESV)

For whatever is born of God overcomes the world; and this is the victory that has overcome the world--our faith. Who is the one who overcomes the world, but he who believes that Jesus is the Son of God?

Day 22

World View

Failure means a lack of success, and society FEEDS on the failure of people. Great things happen all the time. Nevertheless, you will hear more about how people fail than when they succeed.

Self-View

I used to feel like such a failure. I was at an age where I felt like I should have accomplished much more than I had. I was struggling to maintain the American Dream that was consumed by life. Life had become overwhelming, and I was in survival mode.

God's View

Please say the following affirmation:

Everything I need for success is inside of me! I am my greatest asset! The Word of God is the ultimate source of knowledge. I speak

and I believe the Word of God! I am God's trophy and He wants me to shine!

Bible Verse to Remember: Ephesians 2: 7-9 (TPT)

Throughout the coming ages we will be the visible display of the infinite riches of his grace and kindness, which was showered upon us in Jesus Christ. For by grace you have been saved by faith. Nothing you did could ever earn this salvation, for it was the love gift from God that brought us to Christ! So no one will ever be able to boast, for salvation is never a reward for good works or human striving.

DAY 23

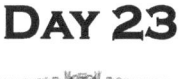

World View

To be broken-hearted means "to be overwhelmed by grief or disappointment". However, comfort means to be "at ease and freedom from pain or distress". It is difficult for society to deal with being heartbroken because we are not taught to handle disappointment and or rejection. In youth sports teams, everyone gets a trophy whether they win or not. Then, they enter society as grownups and can't understand why they didn't get the promotion. Everything is protecting them from pain instead of how to think and put it in its proper place so it doesn't have any power. We give pain power when we don't address it.

Self-View

Today, I needed my mother. I needed her strength. I needed her wisdom that comes with age. I needed to smell her scent. I needed the comfort that only she could bring. We have not spoken in many years. At the time, it was as if our relationship would never be restored. In these tough moments, it would feel like I could almost hear her thick accent. She would say, "Pick yourself up. Have a good cry and talk to your God!" In my longing, I realized that my mother and I are not much different. When adversity rears its ugly head, we both turn to the one who knitted us.

God's View

Please say the following affirmation:

The Lord is close to the broken hearted. I am not alone. I have HOPE.

Bible Verse to Remember: Psalm 34:18 (NIV)

The Lord is close to the brokenhearted and saves those who are crushed in spirit.

Day 24

World View

Have you ever seen a recycling sign? It's a set of arrows that looks like a triangle to represent a cycle: a set of repeating events. This sign is also universally accepted as a way to know what trash can become treasure again. When we give someone an exalted place they don't deserve, we put them on a pedestal. We keep doing the same thing. We get the same results. Then, we wonder why we are so frustrated.

Self-View

I have suffered from childhood into adulthood. I trusted wrong time and time again. I placed people on pedestals. Many of these people did not truly see me. The people we put on pedestals are struggling just like us. They were wading in murky waters. They used what I told them to keep me in a spin cycle. One day, my eyes opened to this vicious cycle.

God's View

Please say the following affirmation:

I will NOT be ignorant of the enemies desires. Father, grant me strategies to overcome and overthrow every plot and plan that is set up for my demise. In Jesus name.

Bible Verse to Remember: 2 Corinthians 2: 11 (TPT)

That no advantage may be gained over us by Satan: for we are not ignorant of his devices.

Day 25

World View

Have you been in traffic and everyone is passing you, but the speed limit is 70 miles per hour? That's today's level of patience. Patience the ability to accept, tolerate, delay trouble or suffering without getting angry or upset. Society now is shopping online, ordering groceries or coffee, picking up dinner, and picking it up in a matter of minutes. We love instant gratification. It keeps getting faster and faster. Delivery now can be within the hour. No one has patience.

Self-View

I wanted so desperately to heal. I was so tired of feeling bad. I wanted to be on a fast track. I wanted expedited healing. I had to tell myself, "Rabia: Be patient with yourself. You are in a rediscovery mode. You are creating deep boundaries to maintain your peace. THE WAR HAS BEEN WON. The battles are daily! I love you, and I accept you. Girl, you are amazing!" God is so invested in our healing! He wants us well.

God's View

Please say the following affirmation:

I abandon my strength and embrace YOUR endurance, Jesus! Jesus, You did not falter. You did not quit. Despite the anguish, You chose us.

Bible Verse to Remember: Hebrews 12:1 (TPT)

As for us, we have all of these great witnesses who encircle us like clouds. So we must let go of every wound that has pierced us and the sin we so easily fall into. Then we will be able to run life's marathon race with passion and determination, for the path has already been marked out before us.

Day 26

World View

If something is complete, it is whole or perfect. It has all the necessary parts to succeed. Pictures these days have to be perfect. That is why there are filters and the trash can icon. Everyone feels like they have to act perfect even if they are nowhere near it. In today's world, perfection and completion have become synonymous when they truly have nothing to do with each other.

Self-View

I felt robbed by choices I had to make to survive. I felt powerless, yet I had a fire raging in me. I had this fire that would burn everything in its path: good or bad. I wanted to put that fire out. Instead, the fire burned brighter and hotter. Eventually, anger consumed me, and I was numb. I was impenetrable. Anger was not a part of my foundation. Then one day, I met a man. He told me God's love is COMPLETE acceptance. He loved me just as I was.

God's View

Please say the following affirmation:

Father,

Thank you that YOU loved me first. Thank You that I was on Your heart all along. Thank You that Your desire is to make me whole. Thank You that I am complete in You. In Jesus name.

Bible Verse to Remember: I John 4:18 (TPT)

Love never brings fear, for fear is always related to punishment. But love's perfection drives the fear of punishment far from our hearts. Whoever walks constantly afraid of punishment has not reached love's perfection.

Day 27

World View

To worry is to allow your mind to dwell on difficulty or troubles. Worry has impacted the stress levels for everyone. Suicide rates and depression have been on the rise. Everyone is in a panic because they fear what they do not know. In a world of certainty, to not know causes a lot of problems.

Self-View

After my divorce, I was really concerned that my children would be affected negatively. I worried about many things from finances to now being a single parent. I wasn't a product of divorce. When I took my vows, I had every intention of "...till death do us part". I would lay in bed consumed with worry and doubt. I questioned if I made the right decision? Then, the God that I served whispered "Cast all your cares on me."

God's View

Please say the following affirmation:

God, I give you all my worries. They belong to you. I cast my cares upon You.

Bible Verse to Remember: 1 Peter 5:7 (NIV)

Cast all your anxiety on him because he cares for you.

Day 28

World View

Society can be so judgmental and they can suck the joy, a feeling of great pleasure and happiness caused by something exceptionally good or satisfying, out of simple things. For example, how many times have you seen someone's picture on social media and they look happy? Then, you read the comments below and the feedback is so negative. It's like they are Joy Sucker Vampires!

Self-View

Most of my life, I have been unhappy. I looked through my Facebook memories and ran across pictures of my past relationships. My smile was bright, but my eyes were dark and full of pain. I felt sorry for myself. However, I also realized that it was my responsibility to be happy. No matter what happens, I make the final decision of happiness or sadness. Joy is greater than happiness. Joy is in the spirit. In order to maintain this joy, you have to keep it stirred up. The bible says that the joy of the

Lord is your strength.

God's View

Please say the following affirmation:

I am born again! I am a child of God! I have the Holy Ghost! I got the life of God in me!

Bible Verse to Remember: I Peter 1:23 (TPT)

For through the eternal and living Word of God you have been born again. And this "seed" that he planted within you can never be destroyed but will live and grow inside of you forever.

Day 29

World View

To surrender means to stop resisting and abandon oneself entirely. In other words, you give yourself up. Surrender in society is seen as a bad thing. No one wants to be controlled. In wars, the side that surrenders is declared the loser. You admit that someone had a better plan or day than you.

Self-View

I laid in bed one morning reflecting about life decisions I made that did not result in success. I realized that God did not require my help. He did not need my input. In order to stop repeating cycles, I had to come to terms with the fact that I needed help that no human could provide.

God's View

Please say the following affirmation:

I refuse to return to the old way of living. I live for Christ who lives in me. He is the author and finisher of my faith. I surrender to you, Jesus.

Bible Verse to Remember: 2 Corinthians 5:17 (NIV)

Therefore, if anyone is in Christ, the new creation has come: The old has gone, the new is here!

Day 30

World View

"Seat belts, please!" We have all heard this while driving. They help us to stay bound or secured to our seats just in case something happens. We have a safety plan in place just in case something goes wrong. While seat belts in cars are great, seat belts in our real life keep us from experiencing truth. They bind us to lies and beliefs that who we are is who we are and we have no room to grow.

Self-View

I was born and raised in Durban, South Africa. I grew up in a very oppressive environment. I asked myself, "Why am I still bound?" I decided that day that I will live free in my latter days. People live their lives as they please/choose. The elderly have lived their lives and want to dictate how I should move! Not anymore! I am no longer bound by culture.

God's View

Please say the following affirmation:

I will live free days, with the Spirit of God as my guide and my internal compass.

Bible Verse to Remember: Romans 8:4 (TPT)

So now every righteous requirement of the law can be fulfilled through the Anointed One living his life in us. And we are free to live, not according to our flesh, but by the dynamic power of the Holy Spirit!

Day 31

World View

Desire is "a strong feeling or wanting to have something or wishing for something to happen". Desire fuels appetites like new cars, new clothes, designer clothes, or a new more expensive home, regardless if you can afford them or not. It can also make you settle for a marriage or a relationship that is less than what you are worthy of.

Self-View

As a child, I learned many amazing things from my mother. One of those things was the discipline to pray. She would wake up daily at 4:30 AM and start her day talking to the Lord. She would then wake us kids up and pray. I complained once about getting up so early, but she modeled a prayer life in front of her kids. I learned the discipline of prayer from a Muslim woman. It may seem strange, but these lessons taught me to seek God first! There are many distractions that could keep us from seeking

God first. We want immediate answers. Life can be brutal, and it can cause us to lose the desire to pray.

God's View

Please say the following affirmation:

Father, I thank you that you are my first desire. Give me a desire for You and Your Word. Keep me hungry Jesus. My desire for you will be unquenchable! In Jesus name!

Bible Verse to Remember: Psalm 37:4 (TPT)

Delight yourself in the Lord, and he will give you the desires of your heart.

Another Letter For You

As you learn to build your confidence in God with these affirmations, we know that you may experience some bumps in the road. Therefore, we hope that you will accept this letter from us to you to remember how blessed you are.

Dear **(Insert Your Name)**,

I'm blessed to know not just **(Insert name)** without anger, but full of grace, kindness, sacrifice and love. The **(insert name)** I know can use this anger against the self-pity, rejection, fear, and the non-irrelevant reflections of the past. The **(insert name)** I know arises and dissipates everything that's against here and him/her God-Given mandate! The **(insert name)** I know arises so that more understanding and the ability to appropriate wisdom to maneuver and Bulldoze forcefully through the cares of life and the distractions of the enemy. I'm confident that this **(insert name)** has already been overcome and it's just a matter of time before the universe gets to acknowledge and know her. I love you, **(insert name)**.

Sincerely,

Me

A Prayer of Salvation

Jesus,

I believe that you died on the cross for me. Forgive me of my sins. Right now, I turn from my sins and open the door of my heart and life to you. I receive you as my Savior to come into my life and save me.

Glossary

- **Stronghold:** A habitual pattern of thought built into one's thought life. Satan and his minions want to capture people's mind because the mind is the citadel of the soul.

- **Overcomer:** A person who succeeds in dealing with or gaining control of some problem or difficulty.

- **Holy Spirit:** The third person of the trinity; God as spiritually active in the world.

- **Prophetic:** Of or relating to foretelling events.

Get connected with Authors Teresa Ngene and Rabia Wood

Teresa Ngene has a great passion to see academic and spiritual growth in children and youth. Her academic and ministry material can be purchased at https://www.teacherspayteachers.com/Store/The-Blooming-Vine.

Rabia has the unique ability to connect with multi-cultural and multi-generational crowds. To hear more from her listen to her on Spotify at The Grace Xperience| Podcast https://open.spotify.com/show/5xVBZnkwpbMNFLrnbfII4h?si=bYBYq9_PQYqWTRvblVhH9g&dl_branch=1&nd=1.

Experiencing Gods Grace

www.ingramcontent.com/pod-product-compliance
Lightning Source LLC
Chambersburg PA
CBHW060851050426
42453CB00008B/938